THE Store Book

by Ronne Peltzman

illustrated by Amye Rosenberg

A Golden Book • New York
Western Publishing Company, Inc., Racine, Wisconsin 53404

 ISBN: 0-307-10086-3 / ISBN: 0-307-68987-5 (lib. bdg.) B C D E F G H I J

SHOPS

On Saturday Amy and Paul went shopping with Mother. They bought lots of things.

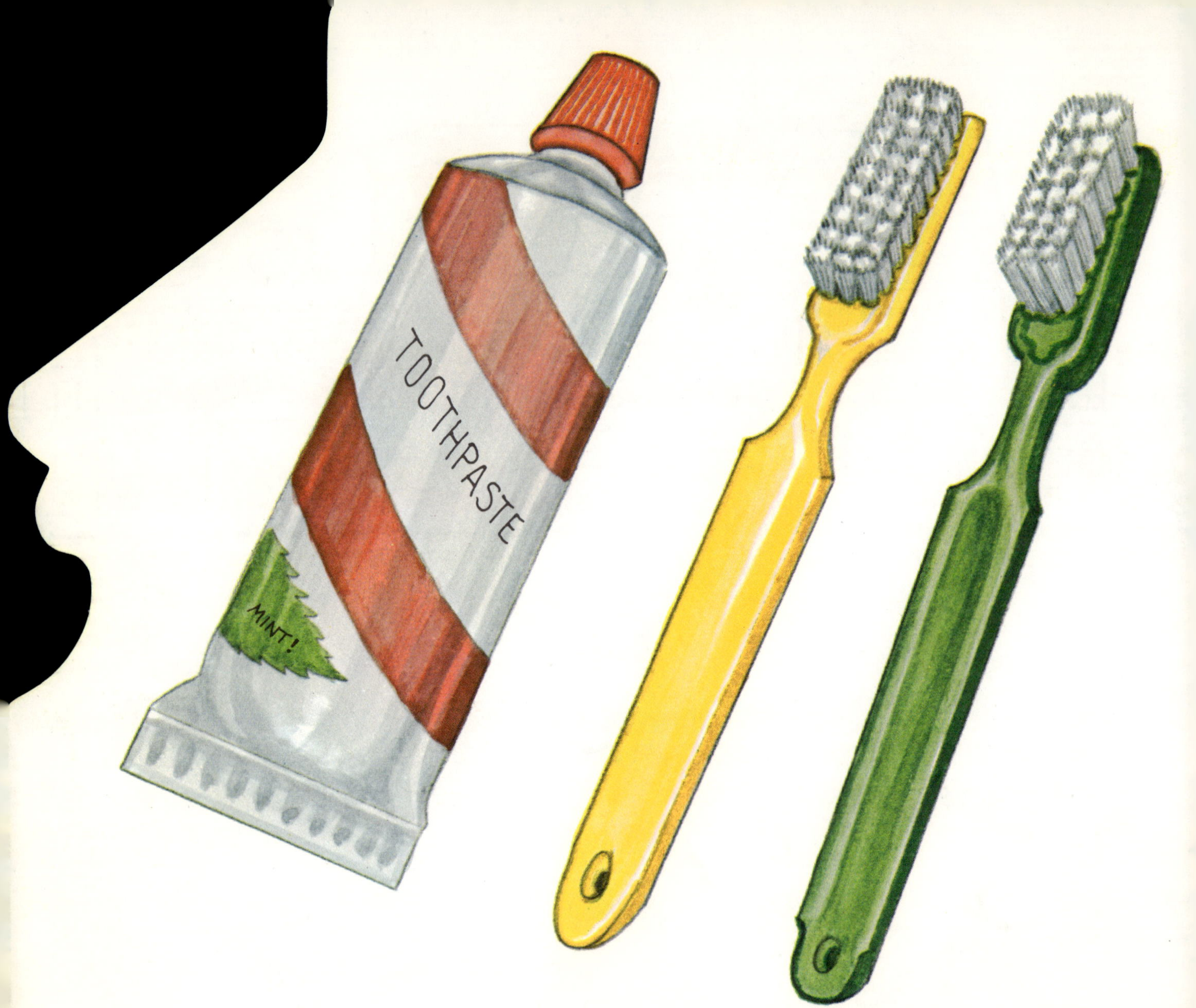

They bought toothpaste and toothbrushes at the drugstore . . .

SALE
TOOTHBRUSHES
NEW!

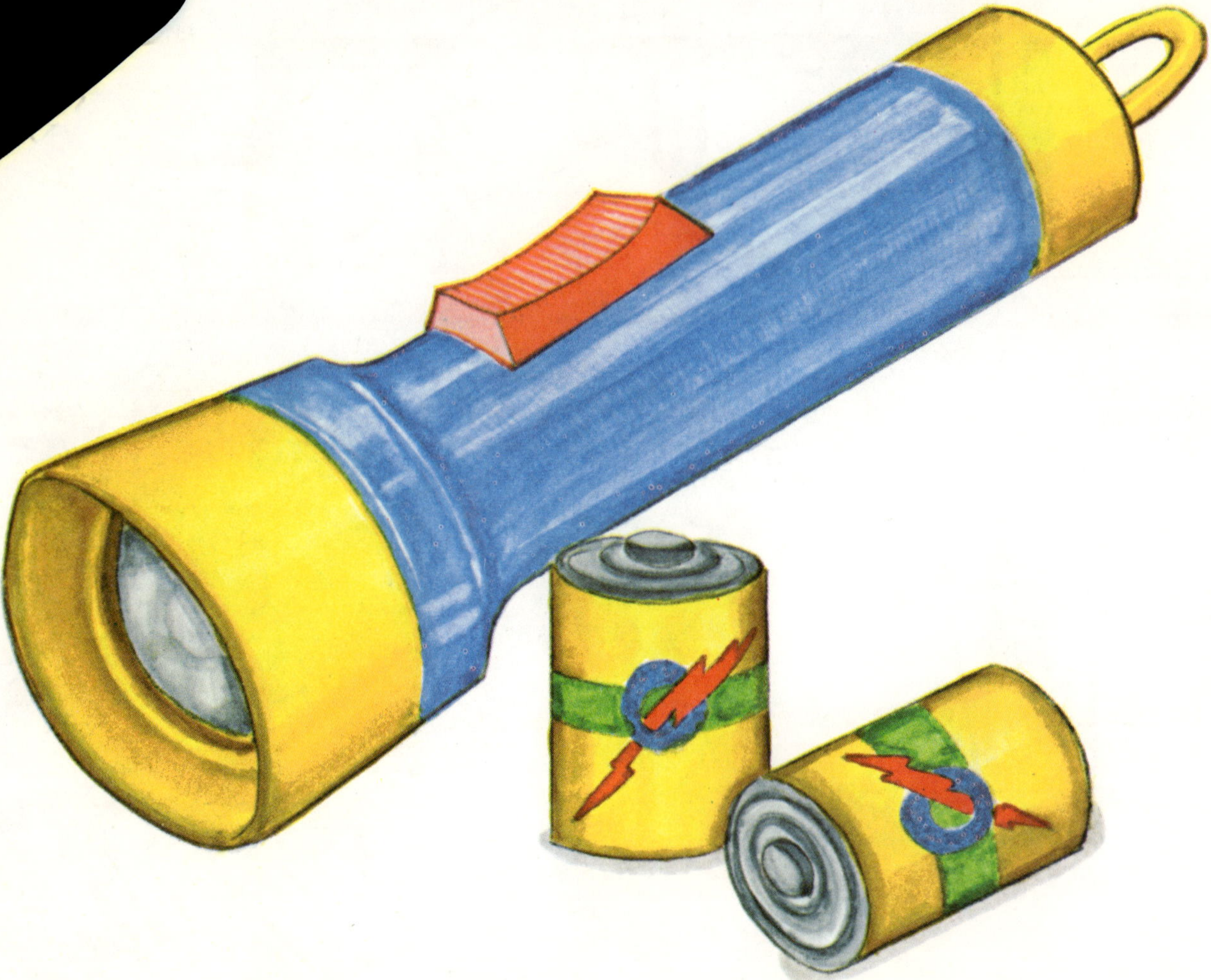

a flashlight at the hardware store . . .

Tools
NUTS 'N BOLTS

T-shirts and socks at the clothing store . . .

SOCKS
9

and new sneakers for school at the shoe store.

Then they had lunch at the diner.

After lunch . . .

they bought a big ABC book at the bookstore . . .

ABC
Animals
BOATS
Birds
Flowers
PLANTS
Peter Rabbit
NEW

a kite and a jack-in-the-box at the toy store . . .

and paper and pencils at the stationery store.

SALE
NEW
PAPER

They also bought orange juice and cereal and peanut butter at the grocery store . . .

COOKIES
CHIPS
CORN FLAKES
PUFFS
CEREAL
OATS
OATS
CEREAL

and carrots and plums at the
fruit-and-vegetable store.

The shopping cart was full. But Mother and Amy and Paul went to one more store on the way home.

It was the ice-cream store.
Guess what they bought there!